America's
NATURAL
WONDERS

America's
NATURAL
WONDERS

TIMOTHY FREW

GALLERY BOOKS
An Imprint of W.H. Smith Publishers, Inc.
112 Madison Avenue
New York, New York 10016

A FRIEDMAN GROUP BOOK

This edition published in 1991 by GALLERY BOOKS
An imprint of W.H. Smith Publishers, Inc.
112 Madison Avenue
New York, New York 10016

ISBN 0-8317-03555

AMERICA'S NATURAL WONDERS
was prepared and produced by
Michael Friedman Publishing Group, Inc.
15 West 26th Street
New York, NY 10010

Editor: Sharon Kalman
Art Director: Jeff Batzli
Designer: Devorah Levinrad
Photography Editor: Christopher Bain

Output by Linographics Corporation
Color separations by Scantrans (Pte.) Ltd.
Printed and bound in Singapore by Tien Wah Press (Pte.) Ltd.

Gallery Books are available for bulk purchase for sales promotions and premium use. For details write or
telephone the Manager of Special Sales, W.H. Smith Publishers, Inc., 112 Madison Avenue,
New York, New York 10016. (212) 532-6600

Acknowledgments

I would like to thank my editor Sharon Kalman and designer Devorah Levinrad of the Friedman Publishing Group for their fine work and their patience. Without them this book would probably never have come to completion. I would also like to thank Loretta McBride, the business manager at Friedman Group for her hard work, which seldom gets acknowledged.

Table of Contents

From the majesty of Niagara Falls and the Mississippi River to the sculpted wastelands of Monument Valley and the Grand Canyon, the North American continent is the rich canvas upon which nature has painted a diverse collection of spectacular phenomena. Virtually every region of the continent contains natural wonders both large and small. The geological forces of nature have worked their magic in many different ways and in many different areas, creating spectacular phenomena that can literally take your breath away and boggle the mind of those who see it for the first time.

Shifting landmasses, meandering rivers, spouting volcanoes, and the wind-blown remains of ancient seabeds—these are the tools which sculpted, shaped, and formed the distinctive North American landscape. Perhaps no other continent possesses such a wide variety of natural wonders. Because of its broad climatic range, North America can at once be home to the sweltering 120 degree F heat of Death Valley, the lowest point in the Western Hemisphere at 282 feet below sea level, and the glacier-sculpted beauty of Denali, the highest peak in the Western Hemisphere at 20,320 feet above sea level.

There are the Badlands, 6,000 square miles of rapidly eroding buttes, cliffs, and gorges; Carlsbad Caverns, ten plus miles of underground caves, decorated with colorful stalactites, stalagmites, and stone draperies; and Assateague, a long, thin barrier island that serves as a bird sanctuary as well as the home of a herd of wild horses.

After 123 years of silence, the once-thought-extinct volcano of Mt. St. Helens blew more then 1,000 feet off of its peak, spewing billions of tons of ash into the air and splintering hundreds of square miles of dense forest in an instant. As destructive as this eruption was, it did serve to show geologists, firsthand, just how the Cascade mountains and other similar mountain ranges were formed.

The geological history of these phenomena is fascinating. Each wonder was formed by several different forces of nature coming together in just the right place, at exactly the right time. Only the perfect combination of soft and hard sedimentary rock—left behind by an extinct sea—combined with the powerful forces of the desert wind could form the giant steeples, buttes, and massifs of Monument Valley. The creviced land and contorted earth of the San Andreas Fault could only occur where two gigantic tectonic plates meet and rub against each other, causing hundreds of years of earthquake activity.

The exact origins of many of these wonders remains a mystery, despite the great strides of science. No matter how advanced geological science becomes, we may never know exactly why the Great Salt Lake was formed, or what factors contributed to the creation of Niagara Falls. Throughout history, man has tried to explain the reasons for what seems inexplicable. The Winnebagos believed that the meandering Wisconsin Dells were created by a giant serpent, making its way south. Those who lived near the beautiful red granite Enchanted Rock in Texas mistook the strange sounds of the cooling rock for ghosts or spirits.

Despite the immensity and seeming timelessness of these wonders, virtually all of them are in a state of constant change. Shifts in climate, the drift of continental plates, and the ongoing process of erosion—the very forces that created these geological marvels—will work to ultimately destroy them. Yet even as these current wonders are diminished, new ones will be created to take their place.

In the meantime, we are left to marvel at their beauty, theorize about their creation, and help protect their future.

ASSATEAGUE ISLAND

LEFT:
The Chincoteague National Wildlife Refuge, on the Virginia portion of the island, serves as a way station for the migratory birds of the Atlantic flyway in the early spring and fall. In addition, the island is home to more than forty different species of shorebirds. The most famous residents of Assateague Island are a herd of wild ponies that live and graze in the grassy marshes. It is believed that these ponies are descendants of a small band of horses left by a shipwrecked Spanish galleon.

LEFT:
Located just eight miles south of Ocean City, Maryland, and two miles east of Chincoteague, Virginia, Assateague Island is a thirty-five-mile-long barrier-reef island made up of wind-sculpted sand dunes, salt marshes, and magnificent white-sand beaches. The island varies in width from just one-third of a mile to more than a mile and is split between Maryland and Virginia.

© Rod Planck/M.L. Dembinsky Photo Assoc.

There are few sensations I prefer to that of galloping over these rolling limitless prairies, rifle in hand, or winding my way among the barren, fantastic and grimly picturesque deserts of the so-called Badlands.
—*Theodore Roosevelt*

∞

Characterized by mile after mile of steep, banded ridges, deep ravines, flat-topped hills, and colorful plateaus, the terrain of the Badlands looks more like the desolate landscape of some far-off planet than it does a national park in the United States. In fact, this South Dakota desert has been used in films and television to portray everything from prehistoric earth to the surface of Mars and post-apocalyptic America.

∞

One look at the Badlands' jagged ridges, canyons of sheer walls, treacherous cliffs, and pointed pinnacles and spires leaves little wonder as to how the six-thousand-square-mile wasteland got its distinctive moniker. The Sioux Indians dubbed this barren area mako sica, *or "bad land." French fur trappers from Canada borrowed from the Sioux name and called the area* les mauvaises terres a traverser, *or "bad lands to cross." Yet, because of all of their desolation, the Badlands possess an almost otherworldly beauty seen nowhere else on the planet. The many layers of sedimentary beds that comprise the area range in color from snowy white to deep pink, orange, and purple.*

ABOVE AND OPPOSITE
PAGE:

*The Badlands are a testament
to the powers of erosion.
Around 80 million years ago,
during the Oligocene epoch,
this region was occupied by a
shallow, sediment-rich sea.*

*Eventually, the same
earthquakes and land shifting
that formed the Rocky
Mountains pushed the seabed
upward, forming a marshy,
rolling prairie. During this
epoch, a large population of
reptiles, mammals, and birds
lived here. As these inhabitants
died off, their remains sank into
the river sediment and soft
marshes; today, this area is rich
in fossils.*

RIGHT:

*Because the Badlands are
almost completely void of
vegetation, the forces of the
wind, freezing temperatures,
and running water are
continually sculpting and
altering the terrain. In fact, the
erosion process is happening so
quickly that distinct changes
can be seen in the terrain from
year to year.*

© J. Messerschmidt/FPG International

Despite its name, the 36,007-acre national park known as Bryce Canyon is not actually a single canyon at all, but a series of small canyons, cliffs, and ravines. While much of the landscape was formed by tributaries of the Paria River, most of this stone wonderland was sculpted from erosive forces of the wind, rain, and freezing temperatures.

∞

This Utah landmark was named after local rancher Ebenezer Bryce, who once described the series of canyons as "a hell of a place to lose a cow." The canyons run along a twenty-mile section on the eastern edge of the Paunsaugunt Plateau, which is composed of layers of shale, sandstone, and limestone. Mixed in with the sedimentary stone are vast quantities of colored minerals.

The jagged spires, arches, and cathedral formations of Bryce possess an impressive, colorful palette that seems to move with the shifting sunlight. Iron compounds produce the fiery reds, copper creates the rich greens, and manganese compounds produce the deep purples.

∞

Like the Badlands, Bryce Canyon was once an ancient sea. The shifting of the Paunsaugunt Plateau, however, raised the seabed and exposed the fragile rock formations to the forces of erosion. Of the many highly recognizable rock formations and canyons contained in the national park, the most frequently visited and famous are Wall Street, Temple of Osiris, Thor's Hammer, the Camel, and Wise Man.

CARLSBAD CAVERNS

Located in the Chihuahuan Desert in the foothills of the Guadalupe Mountains in New Mexico, the two-hundred-million-year-old Carlsbad Caverns are perhaps the country's most astonishing underground wonder. The cave is made up of a series of "rooms" filled with hundreds of colorful stalagmites, stalactites, draperies, and other formations. Seven of the ten explored miles of the caverns are open to the general public, yet no one knows exactly how deeply into the Guadalupe Mountains the caverns actually descend.

∞

The most famous attractions in Carlsbad Caverns are the Green Lake Room, featuring a pool of water surrounded by stalagmites; the Papoose Room, known for its gigantic stone draperies; the Queen's Chamber, a small room 829 feet below the surface; and the aptly named Big Room. Covering more than fifteen acres, the Big Room is a two-hundred-foot-high chamber containing such spectacular formations as the Twin Domes, Rock of Ages, Totem Pole, and the Giant Dome, a massive column rising to sixty-two feet and spanning more than two hundred feet.

∞

The first recorded discovery of the caverns was by an unnamed southwestern cowhand in the late 1800s. Many years later, explorers found the remains of a sandal believed to be from the Indian Basket Maker culture, nearly four thousand years ago. Carlsbad was originally named the Bat Cave because every night from April to October, hundreds of thousands of bats emerge from the cavern at sunset and fly all night to the valleys of the Pecos and Black rivers, where they feed on moths, beetles, and other insects. These bats cover an average of 150 miles on their nocturnal journey before returning to the cave at sunrise to sleep all day.

The first commercial use of the cave was as a source of nitrate-rich bat guano. More than one hundred thousand tons of guano were removed from the cave for use as fertilizer in the twenty years before its establishment as a national monument in 1923.

(Iowa)

CRATERS OF THE MOON

ABOVE AND OPPOSITE PAGE:

*The Craters of the Moon
National Monument is an
eerily beautiful collection of
caves, natural bridges, cones,
terraces, and mounds of
volcanic stone that resemble the
cratered surface of the moon.
This unusual natural wonder is
the result of three periods of
intense volcanic eruption, the
most recent of which took place
about 1,000 years ago. Boiling
lava at temperatures of up to
2,000 degrees F seeped up
through the cracks and vents in
the granite. A sea of molten
rock literally flooded over the
countryside before gradually
cooling and seeping back down
into the black caves. Billions of
tons of lava flowed out of the
ground in this relatively small
section of what is now Blaine
and Butte counties in Iowa.
The lava erupted with such
force that huge blocks of
unmelted rock were torn from
the ceiling of underground lava
reservoirs and carried to the
surface like driftwood.*

RIGHT:

*As the lava cooled it formed the
unusual, otherworldly
formations that gave the area its
name. The most famous
formations are Devils Orchard,
Big Cinder Cone, Sunset Cone,
Silent Cone, North Crater, Big
Crater, and a gigantic crack
known simply as the Great Rift.*

The lava is made up mostly of iron-rich basalt. In the bright sunlight the rock looks almost like polished blue or black glass. This lava forms gigantic black buttes, rippled, hardened seas of solid rock, ribbons of stone, and hundreds of caverns, tunnels, and pits. Some of the caves here hold water that never rises more than 2 degrees above freezing, even on the hottest days.

∞

Set aside as a national monument in 1924, this eighty-square-mile area is actually part of a larger field that covers nearly 200,000 square miles and extends west to the Columbia Plateau. One of the largest national monuments in North America, Craters of the Moon was not thoroughly explored until about thirty years ago.

© Stephen Trimble

DEATH VALLEY

*A depressed basin in Inyo
County, California, Death
Valley is the lowest point on the
North American continent and
one of the hottest regions in the
world. In the summer,
temperatures regularly go as
high as 120 degrees F and rarely
dip below 70 degrees F. The
entire valley rests below sea
level, dipping to 280 feet below
at its nadir. By contrast, less
than eighty miles due east of
Death Valley is the 14,495-foot
peak of Mount Whitney, one of
the highest points in the
United States.*

The entire valley, whose name commemorates a party of gold prospectors, or "forty-niners," who died of starvation and exposure here in the mid-1800s, covers an area of about fifty by twenty miles, just north of the Mojave Desert, reaching east of the Sierra Nevadas on into Nevada. As beautiful as it is desolate, Death Valley is characterized by wind-worn rock formations, ever-changing sand dunes, and a crusted surface containing extensive deposits of salt, borax, and sodium nitrate. Adding to the mystique of the valley's name is the Amargosa River, the final channel of an extensive California drainage system that enters the valley and then simply disappears in the basin.

(Alaska)
MT. McKINLEY
DENALI

Denali is a word from the Athabascan Indian language that translates as "the high one"—and you need not wonder why. Formerly known as Mount McKinley, Denali reaches 20,300 feet at its peak, making it the highest point on the American continent. In fact, the summit of Denali is so high that it is literally shrouded in clouds and fog more than 60 percent of the time.

In 1917, President Woodrow Wilson designated Denali and the area surrounding it as a national park. The park was enlarged in 1922 and again in 1932, when it reached its current size of two million acres, making it the second-largest National Park in North America, next to Yellowstone.

∞

The entire six-hundred-mile Alaska Range was formed from the Denali Fault System, the largest crustal break in all of North America. Millions of years ago the two opposing landmasses met, one pushing the other into the earth, while raising itself high into the sky. During the last Ice Age, heavy glacial activity sculpted both the mountains and the surrounding land. The result is Alaska's distinctive razor-edged ridges, saw-toothed spires, U-shaped valleys, and saucer lakes.

∞

© John Shaw/Tom Stack & Associates

The towering giant is made even more impressive when compared to its surroundings. In the Alaska Range, where Denali sits, there are fewer than twenty peaks that exceed ten thousand feet. Four of the highest peaks in the range are contained in the 3,030-square-mile Denali national park: Mount Mather, 12,123 feet; Mount Crosson, 12,800 feet; Mount Silverthorn, 13,220 feet; and Mouth Foraker, 17,400 feet.

© Galen Rowell/FPG International

FAR LEFT:

The colossal, flat-topped, fluted stone formation known simply as Devils Tower juts out of the ground in one of Wyoming's most isolated regions. Located in a forested area along the Belle Fourche River, twenty-five miles north of Sundance and seventy miles west of Deadwood, Devils Tower can be seen from a distance of more than one hundred miles. And no wonder; the natural stone tower rises 869 feet from the forest floor and has a diameter of more than one thousand feet at its base.

∞

Essentially a formation of rock columns, the tower dates back some 50 million years, when volcanic eruptions propelled the huge shaft of molten rock up through the floor of an ocean. As the volcanic rock cooled, it assumed its now familiar columnar appearance. Eventually, the ocean receded and the powers of the wind and the rain sculpted the masterpiece.

ABOVE:

On September 24, 1906, the United States government established Devils Tower and the surrounding 1,200 acres as the country's first national monument. Along with scores of sight-seeing tourists, the monument is visited yearly by rock-climbing enthusiasts from around the world, anxious to test their skills on this monolith.

© Thomas Kitchin/Tom Stack & Associates

DINOSAUR PROVINCIAL PARK

Located along the banks of the Red River in Alberta, Canada, Dinosaur Provincial Park is a barren badland that rivals those in neighboring Montana (Pine Butte Preserve) and South Dakota (Badlands National Park) in both size and beauty. In fact, all three of these badlands are a result of the same prehistoric sea. Over 80 million years ago, a sprawling 130,000-square-mile sea covered large portions of present-day Alberta, Saskatchewan, Manitoba, Montana, and the Dakotas, depositing thick layers of sediment. The same cataclysmic land shift that raised the Rocky Mountains drained the sea away and formed rolling hills and broad valleys.

∞

As with Pine Butte Preserve and the Badlands, Dinosaur Provincial Park has some of the richest Cretaceous fossil beds in the world, with some specimens dating back as far as 76 million years. Within the past century, paleontologists have uncovered the fossilized remains of Parasaurolophus, Corythosaurus, Albertosaurus, Stenonychosaurus, and many more. In addition, fossils of warm-blooded mammals from later periods have been found in the area: the saber-toothed tiger, the camel, and the three-toed horse are just a few examples.

Between 64 and 76 million years ago the area that is now Dinosaur Provincial Park was covered with vast swamps and marshes. The chief inhabitants of these fertile wetlands were the great dinosaurs. They roamed this area for millions of years before dying off and sinking into the swamp.

∞

Volcanic activity from the Yellowstone region soon covered the area with volcanic ash. Over the past several million years the area has been in a constant state of erosion, as strong winds and rain break away the soft sandstone and brittle shale.

(Texas)
ENCHANTED ROCK

At night, the Comanche Indians who inhabited the lands around what is now Llano, Texas, would hear a strange howling and whistling coming from the huge outcropping of pink granite nearby. The sounds did not come from any animal, or in fact, from anything living. A legend soon developed that the rock was haunted by spirits who would only appear at night, and only during the hottest parts of the summer. The Comanches called the huge piece of granite, Enchanted Rock.

∞

In fact, the strange noises the Native Americans heard were not caused by spirits but by the contracting and shifting of the rock itself as it cooled at night.

ABOVE:
*Located a few miles north of the
historic German community of
Fredricksburg, Texas,
Enchanted Rock is a rugged
outcropping of eroded red
granite surrounded by a mass
of scattered boulders. One of the
largest outcroppings of granite
in North America, this smooth,
weather-polished dome rises
more than 500 feet from the bed
of Sand Creek, at its base.
Around the foot of the rock lies
a collection of granite boulders
and fragments, some as large as
a house, as well as granite
domes, towers, turrets,
battlements, and walls.*

The scene is so weird and lonely and so incomprehensible in its novelty that one feels that it could never have been viewed before.
—*Frederick S. Dellenbaugh*
The Romance of the
Colorado River

∞

This is a warm place. I fainted when I saw that awful-looking canyon. I never wanted a drink so bad in my life....
—*Gertrude B. Stevens*
from an 1892 guest book

∞

Perhaps no other location on earth is as astonishing and awe-inspiring as the Grand Canyon. Visitors who step up to the south rim for the first time are literally dumbfounded by the spectacular, multicolored peaks and cliffs that seem to fall away into eternity. All sense of visual perspective is suddenly lost as landmarks that are miles away seem close enough and vivid enough to touch. Francisco de Coronado, who lived in the sixteenth century and was one of the canyon's first European explorers, wrote of trying "to find a passage down to the river, which looked from above as if the water was six feet across, although the Indians said it was half a league wide." To confound things even more, as the hot Arizona sun moves across the sky, all perspective changes with the shifting shadows.

At Granite Gorge, its deepest point, the canyon wall drops away for a full mile. And along its 217-mile length, the canyon varies in width from four to eighteen miles. At the bottom of the world's largest gorge is the Grand Canyon's sculptor, the Colorado River. To put its immense size in perspective, the Grand Canyon covers more than two thousand square miles, about the size of Delaware.

∞

The walls of the Grand Canyon represent a geological timetable. The rocks at the bottom of granite gorge date back some two billion years, to the Precambrian era, when the earth's molten core burst upward and punctured the surface. In contrast, the uppermost layers of shale, sandstone, and limestone are a mere 600 million years old, and were deposited there as sediment on the bottom of a Paleozoic-era ocean.

The actual formation of the canyon itself is much more recent. About two million years ago, the Colorado River narrowed and increased in force as a terrestrial upheaval pushed rocks from northern Arizona and southern Utah toward it. Gradually, the river began to erode the soft upper layers of rock. As it dug deeper, the surrounding land was raised, essentially locking the river into a single course and thus increasing its erosive powers.

∞

In 1858, Lieutenant Joseph Ives took a steamer named Explorer from the Gulf of California up the Colorado River in order to explore the territory northwest of Arizona. Eventually, Ives and his men had to abandon the steamer and continued overland, where they came across the "Big Canyon of the Colorado." Despite its obvious grandeur, Ives saw the canyon as nothing more than a wasteland: "Ours has been the first, and will doubtless be the last party of whites to visit this profitless locality. It seems intended by nature that the River Colorado, along the greater part of its lonely and majestic way, shall be forever unvisited and undisturbed."

∞

Ives could not have been more wrong. Every year hundreds of thousands of people visit this "profitless locality," making it the most popular natural attraction in the world. And with little wonder—few sights are as spectacular and breathtaking as the "Big Canyon of the Colorado" at sunset.

(Utah)

GREAT SALT LAKE

The remnant of a prehistoric inland sea known as Lake Bonneville, the Great Salt Lake is the saltiest body of water other than the Dead Sea. In fact, its saline content is roughly six times that of any ocean in the world, making it a safe haven for even the most inexperienced swimmers. The water here is so dense with salt that a human being simply cannot sink below the surface.

∞

Lake Bonneville was formed from glacial runoff after the last Ice Age. This enormous lake was about twenty times the size of the Great Salt Lake—covering what is now northwest Utah, eastern Nevada, and southern Idaho—and reached a maximum depth of about one thousand feet.

The constant loss of water due to evaporation eventually shrunk the lake to its current size, while concentrating the mineral salts brought in by its three feeder rivers: the Jordan, the Bear, and the Weber.

∞

For the most part, the Great Salt Lake has been shrinking over the past few hundred years, despite the fact that it has three rivers feeding it and no outlet. Land development around the lake, as well as irrigation systems along the feeder rivers, have dramatically increased the evaporation rate. In fact, since 1850 the lake has shrunk from 1,750 square miles to about 1,500 square miles. Of course, as the lake shrinks, the saline content of the water goes up. At present, salt levels fluctuate from 18 to 25 percent.

OVERLEAF:
Ten miles long and fifty miles wide, the Great Salt Lake contains numerous islands of varying sizes. Many of these islands and a lot of the shoreline, however, become flooded during wet years, when there is heavy snow runoff from the surrounding mountains. This flooding can create major problems for the local populations of bison and gulls.

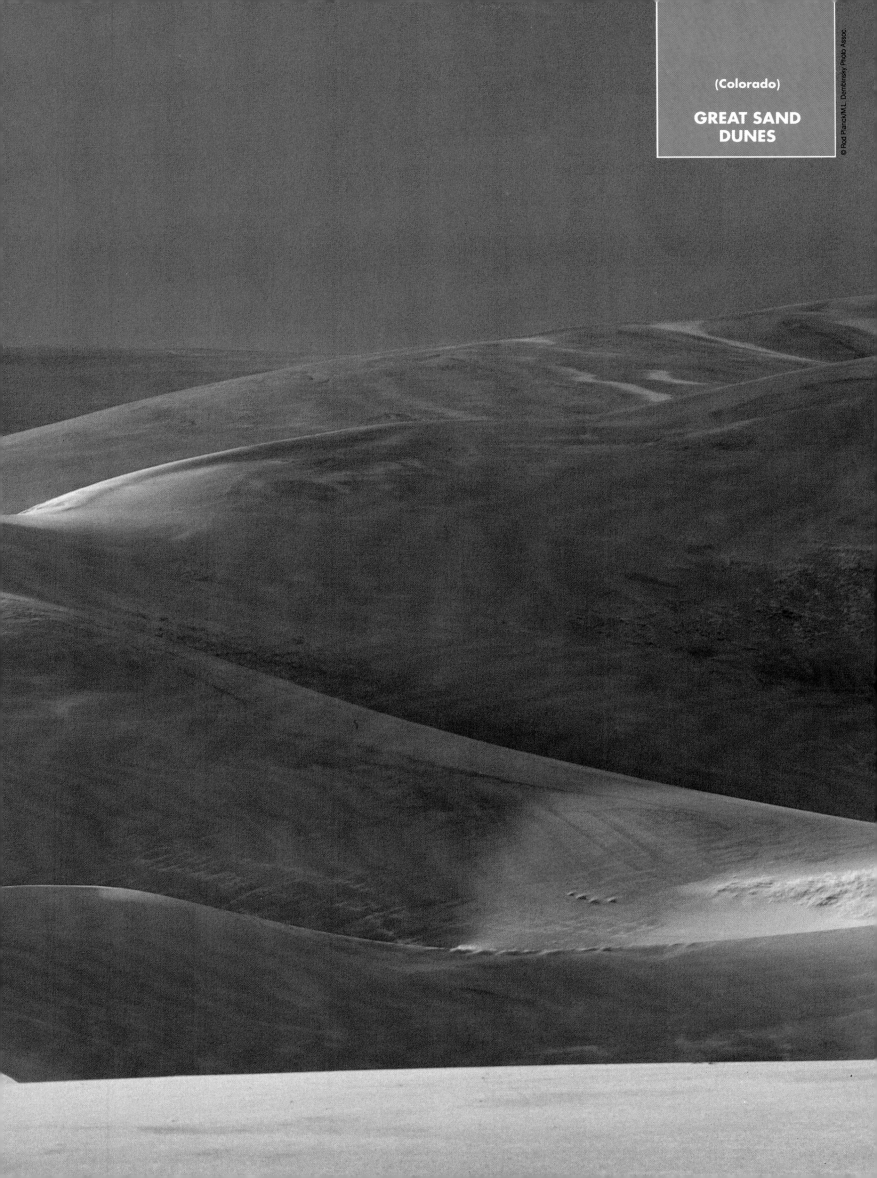

PREVIOUS PAGE:
Colorado. When one thinks of this state, images of towering conifers, snowcapped mountains, and clear, cold-running streams come to mind. Yet here, nestled between the Sangre de Cristo Mountains and the San Luis Valley in the southern part of the state sit the Great Sand Dunes National Monument. To say that this fifty-square-mile area looks out of place is an understatement. With its five hundred-foot-high hills of wavy, wind-sculpted sand, the area looks as if someone grafted a large section of the Sahara Desert to the edge of a snow-capped mountain.

ABOVE:
The dunes have been formed over the past several thousand years as the water and wind scour the surrounding mountains, breaking much of the rock down into sand. The sand is blown or carried by rivers down into the valley, where the prevailing winds carry it northeast to the Sangre de Cristo Mountains. Rising four thousand feet above the valley floor, the Sangre de Cristos cut the wind and force it to drop the sand, thus forming the dunes. The surrounding mountains also make the area very susceptible to violent thunderstorms. In fact, the visitors' center boasts exhibits of sand that have been fused into hard, glassy rocks by the lightning.

RIGHT:
It is not surprising that North America's major rain forest system would lie in the moisture-laden Pacific Northwest. Trade winds sweep eastward across the Pacific Ocean for two thousand miles before hitting the massive obstacle posed by the Olympic Mountains. There they cool and drop between 150 and two hundred inches of rain every year into the Bogachiel, Queets, Wuinault, and Hoh valleys, forming a network of dense rain forests—the most famous of which is the Hoh.

LEFT:
The Hoh Rain Forest is a luxurious green woodland that rivals any tropical jungle for beauty and wildlife. Here, thousand-year-old trees tower three hundred feet high above the dense carpet of moss and ferns that make up the forest floor. Virgin spruce and hemlock form the evergreen canopy and seal in moisture so that the spiraling vine maples and club moss can thrive below and climb up their trunks.

RIGHT AND BELOW:
As with most rain forests, the soil beneath the Hoh has been depleted of most of its nutrient value. The dense vegetation in the area literally feeds upon itself. As foliage dies and falls to the ground, it decomposes and provides the necessary nutrients for the forest to survive. Among the hundreds of varieties of mosses, shrubs, lichens, liverworts, and fungi present in the Hoh are huckleberry, oxalis, vanilla leaf, bedstraw, bunchberry, skunk cabbage, and fern.

(Arkansas)

HOT SPRINGS

Located in Arkansas' Ouachita Mountains, Hot Springs was essentially America's first health spa. Long before the first white man set foot in the area, Native Americans considered these "miracle waters" neutral ground where all tribes were welcome. The Native Americans believed the forty steaming springs held strong curative powers and bathed there to relieve themselves of a wide variety of ailments.

∞

The water averages about 143 degrees F year round, and about 850,000 gallons bubble up through the springs every day. It starts as rainwater that seeped deeply into the ground. While underground, the water is heated by the earth's inner core and is then forced back up through a fault in the crust. The entire process, from rainfall to spring water, can take anywhere from twenty years to four thousand years.

THE HUDSON BAY

The Hudson Bay is a large inland sea, connected on the east to the Atlantic Ocean by way of the Hudson Strait and on the north to the Arctic Sea by way of Foxe Channel and Fury and Hecla straits.

∞

Henry Hudson's namesake bay covers some seven hundred thousand square miles, including neighboring James Bay and Foxe Channel. Throughout much of the year the bay remains frozen, limiting safe navigation from July to October.

∞

In the southern sections of the bay, balsam, spruce, and poplar grow, making a beautiful and inviting home for musk ox and caribou as well as ducks, geese, ptarmigan, and loons. The waters of the bay itself support a healthy fish population of cod, lake trout, and salmon, as well as a few porpoise and whales.

Except for several bands of Eskimo and a few resourceful Canadians, the majority of the Hudson Bay remains isolated, untouched wilderness.

∞

On April 17, 1610, Henry Hudson sailed from London aboard a small ship named Discovery toward the New World, in his fourth and final attempt to find the Northwest Passage to China. The determined Hudson sailed steadily westward and eventually entered the strait that now bears his name. On August 3, the Discovery entered the waters of the Hudson Bay. Henry Hudson was so enamored of the bay that he spent nearly three months exploring its eastern shore.

(California)

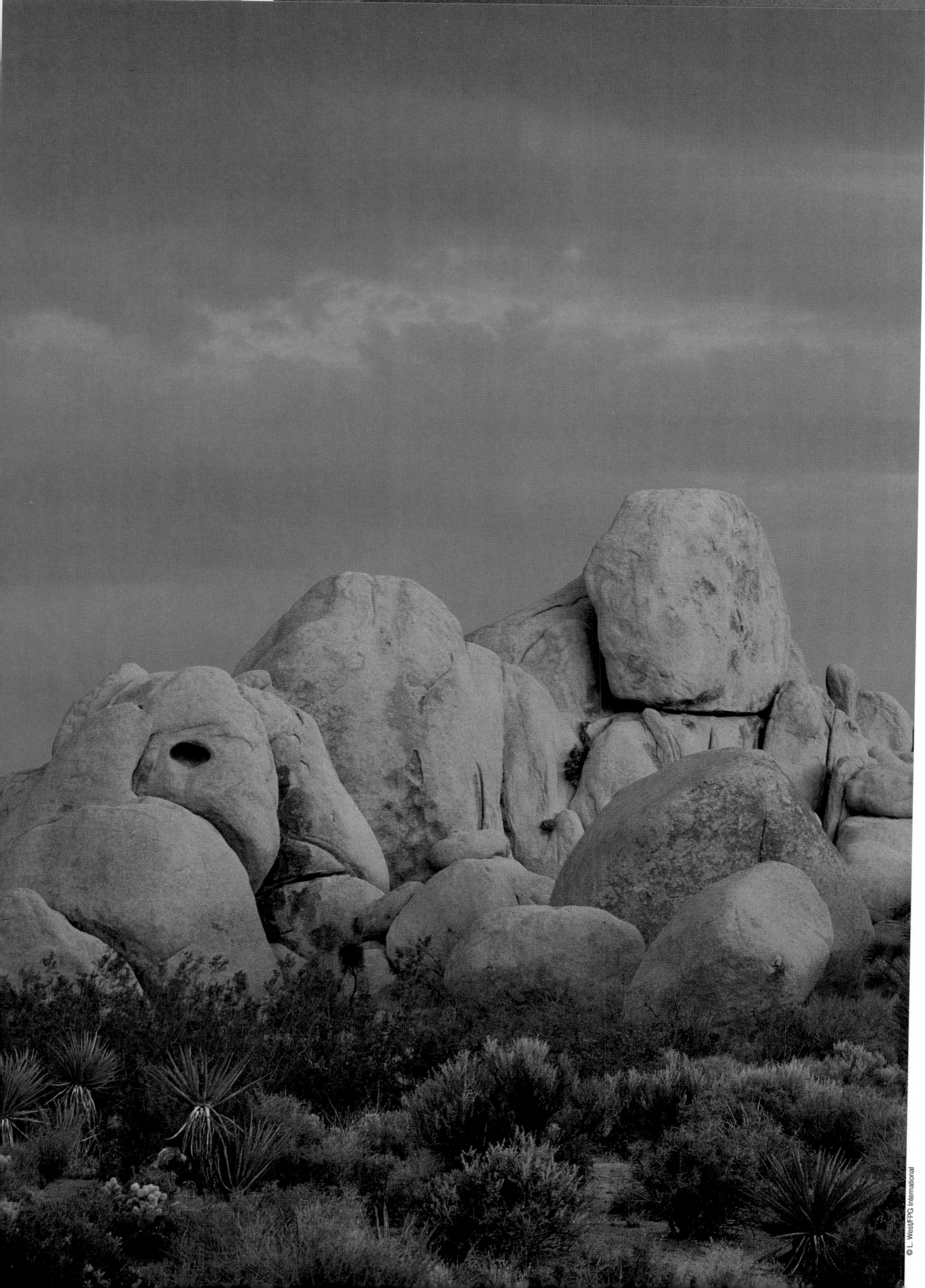

LEFT:
The Joshua Tree National Monument contains a rich array of desert flora, animal life, and stunning, wind-carved granite formations.
The area gets its name from a gigantic, endangered yucca, called the Joshua tree. A member of the agave family, the Joshua tree can attain a height of forty feet or more. Its thick, tangled branches bear eight- to ten-inch-long clusters of cream-white blossoms.

LEFT AND OPPOSITE PAGE:
Like other yuccas, the Joshua tree can survive under adverse conditions: The area in which it grows averages less than six inches of rainfall a year and has temperatures that regularly rise above 100 degrees F.

Even in the monument bearing its name, the Joshua tree is scarce. It can only be found in the central section of the park, where the altitude is three thousand feet above sea level.

(Hawaii)

KILAUEA CRATER

PREVIOUS PAGE:

The Kilauea volcano in Hawaii Volcanoes National Park can be seen almost as the antithesis of areas such as the Badlands and the Grand Canyon. While the two latter areas are in a constant state of disintegration—victims of the relentless forces of wind, temperature, and water— Kilauea regularly adds to the size and the shape of Hawaii, the island it helped to form.

∞

Along with its neighboring Mauna Loa, Kilauea is among the most active volcanoes in the world. In fact, it has erupted every year except two since 1959. The result of all of this activity has been the addition of nearly one billion cubic yards of lava to the island.

© Stephen Trimble

ABOVE:

One of the best ways to understand the awesome power of the volcano is to walk down Devastation Trail, a half mile of boardwalk on top of the cinders and through a burned-out forest.

RIGHT:

The island of Hawaii, like the other islands in the chain, began as a fissure in the ocean floor nearly three million years ago, although it is believed that the peaks did not break the sea's surface until five hundred thousand years ago. Hawaii also sits in the middle of the Pacific Plate, which is slowly moving northwest. Beneath the island and the plate is the volcano's fissure, or "hot spot"—the vent through which molten lava pours. As the islands form through volcanic activity, they gradually move northwest along with the Pacific Plate. At one time the mountains and islands to the northwest were directly over this vent. Eventually, Kilauea will also be pushed northward and the volcano will cease to be active.

© Stephen Trimble

(Kentucky)
MAMMOTH CAVE

Nearly 240 million years ago, a sea covered what is now Warren County, Kentucky, creating layers of limestone and sandstone. Much later, the shifting of the land caused the seas to drain, seeping through cracks in the earth's crust and eating away at the soft stone underneath. This process of erosion continued for millions of years, forming and reforming the huge system of underground caves known today as Mammoth Cave.

∞

At present, more than 150 miles of the Mammoth Cave system have been explored, yet it is believed that there may be two hundred more miles of unexplored caves linking the system with others in the area. The latest major discovery came in 1972, when a link was found between Mammoth and the nearby Flint Ridge Cave.

∞

In 1935, explorers discovered the remains of "Lost John," the earliest known visitor to Mammoth Cave. It is believed that "John" was mining for gypsum when a loose boulder fell on him, nearly 2,300 years ago.

From a distance, Meteor Crater appears to be nothing more than a small hill in the middle of Arizona. From above, however, it is a remarkable, saucer-shaped opening in the earth, 4,200 feet in diameter and 575 feet deep at its center.

∞

When first discovered in 1871, the crater was believed to be the result of an ancient volcano, much like the nearby Sunset Crater. Twenty years later, mineralogists discovered iron and diamond fragments, leading them to believe that a gigantic meteor had caused the gaping hole. Later, scientists determined that the crater was formed by a meteor and not through volcanic activity.

∞

It is estimated that the meteor was about eighty feet in diameter, weighed seventy thousand tons, and traveled at a velocity of nearly thirty thousand miles per hour. The force of the collision was roughly equivalent to six hundred thousand tons of TNT, or about thirty times the blasts that leveled the Japanese cities of Hiroshima and Nagasaki in World War II.

RIGHT:

The Mississippi is the central trunk of North America's largest river system. It gets its name from the Algonquin Indians, who called it missi sipi, *or "great river." Along with its hundreds of tributaries, the river serves as the main drainage channel for approximately one-eighth of North America (1,300,000 square miles). In addition, the Mississippi's basin occupies two-fifths of the continental United States' total land area.*

© Steve Berman/FPG International

RIGHT:

This great river has played an integral part of the history and development of the United States. The water and soil carried by the Mississippi have made the midwestern section of North America, such places as St. Louis, Missouri, a fertile heartland and the center for the grain, cattle, and textile industries. In the early days of American settlement, before the heyday of the railroads, the river served as a major transportation link between the economic center of Chicago and the rest of the American heartland to the south.

© Mark E. Gibson

Although well known to the Native Americans for hundreds of years, the Mississippi River was first visited by a European when the explorer Hernando de Soto discovered it in 1541. The mighty Mississippi, however, was not visited by another European for more than a century, when Louis Jolliet and Father Jacques Marquette, two French explorers, entered the upper Mississippi from Lake Michigan in 1673. Ten years later, Rene-Robert Cavelier began extensive explorations of the lower portion of the river, and soon the Mississippi began to appear on maps of North America. Today, it is one of the most important waterways in North America.

∞

. . . a yellow-and-purple corrugated world of distance.
—Zane Grey

OPPOSITE PAGE:
The Searchers, Stagecoach, She Wore a Yellow Ribbon, My Darling Clementine, Fort Apache . . . *Anyone who has ever seen a classic John Ford Western is familiar with the grandiose, epic qualities of Monument Valley. Over the years, this stretch of desert straddling the Utah-Arizona border has been the scene of twenty-five movies depicting the myth of the Old West.*

∞

The valley gets its name from its now-famous blocks of red sandstone, or monuments, that reach heights of one thousand feet or more above the desert floor. Ford said he originally chose this location for his first Western, Stagecoach, because the red monuments reminded him of ancient Greek temples standing watch over a long-lost civilization.

(Arizona)

**MONUMENT
VALLEY**

The forces of erosion have been shaping and reshaping the face of the desert. Canyons and gullies were first formed, and eventually even these were whittled down until they took on their present shape.

ABOVE:
More than 200 million years ago, Monument Valley was a flat, windswept, red-sand desert soon to be inundated by an encroaching sea. With the sea came large deposits of sediments, which formed shale and compressed the red sand into sandstone. When the sea receded about 65 million years ago, it left behind a huge, flat plateau of shale-covered sandstone.

RIGHT:

Against the wide Arizona sky, the monuments seem otherworldly. Visitors can't help but compare them to man-made architectural forms such as pillars, chimneys, spires, castles, and temples. In fact, many of the names of the more famous monuments are simply interpretations of what they look like. Two Mittens, for example, are neighboring formations, each with a narrow "thumb" of rock protruding from its side. Castle Rock is a jagged butte topped with fortlike crenellations. And Hen-in-a-Nest looks like a hen sitting on her eggs.

© Stan Osolinski/M.L. Dembinsky Photo Assoc.

RIGHT:

During the sixteenth century, Monument Valley was populated by many members of the huge Navajo tribe. For nearly one hundred years the Navajo lived in and around the valley, largely undisturbed, herding their goats and sheep. Unfortunately for the Navajo, the white man entered the area in the beginning of the seventeenth century. With the white man came confrontation. In 1864, after a long war, the Navajo were defeated and transported to Fort Sumner in New Mexico. Six years later, however, a delegation of Navajo, led by Chief Manuelito, went to Washington to regain their former homeland.

Today, the Navajo still occupy the "place among the red rocks," where they herd their sheep and create turquoise and silver jewelry, mainly for the many tourists who visit the valley and surrounding areas.

© Barbara Von Hoffmann/Tom Stack & Associates

© Kevin Schafer/Tom Stack & Associates

Running from Northern California through Oregon and Washington to the edge of the Fraser River valley and the interior plateau in southern British Columbia, the Cascade Mountains are known for their towering peaks and scenic beauty. The abundant precipitation in the area supports dense forests of Douglas fir, true fir, hemlock, and cedar. These beautiful alpine forests have long attracted tourists and nature lovers to the thousands of square miles of national park lands contained within the mountain range.

∞

All of the peaks of the southern Cascades are of volcanic origin. Thousands of years of volcanic eruptions where the Gorda plate meets the North American Plate have built these towering mountains. The ash and lava flows from this range are largely responsible for the lava fields that cover Oregon, Washington, and Idaho, as well as the volcanic deposits of Yellowstone National Park. For years it was believed that all of the volcanic peaks of the Cascades were extinct, except for perhaps Mount Lassen.

∞

No less beautiful than its larger cousins, the relatively low peak of Mount St. Helens (10,354 feet) was nonetheless far less popular and well known than the more famous Mount Rainier (14,408 feet), Mount Shasta (14,161 feet), and Mount Hood (11,245 feet).

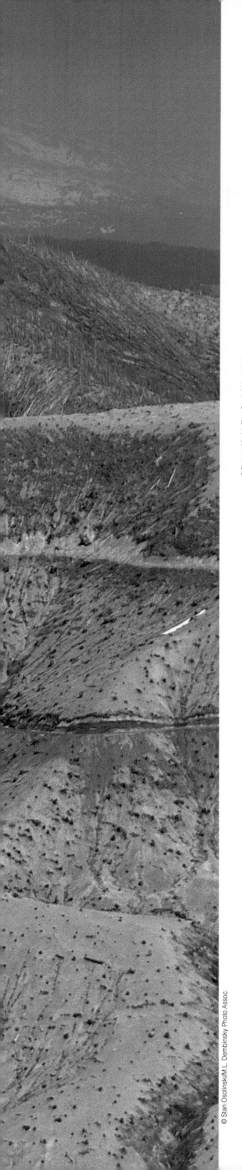

At 8:32 a.m. on May 18, 1980 however, all of that changed. After 123 years of dormancy, Mount St. Helens literally blew its top. Accompanied by an earthquake measuring 5 on the Richter scale, Mount St. Helens erupted, blowing approximately 1,300 feet off the top of the volcano. One hundred and fifty square miles of dense forest was instantly reduced to kindling. A huge plume of ash spewed from the top of the mountain, quickly spreading across the sky and completely obscuring the sun for 150 miles to the north and east. Large sections of Washington, Idaho, and Montana were covered with several inches of ash. Thick mudflows filled the valleys surrounding the volcano, carrying millions of tons of debris into the Toutel and Columbia rivers.

∞

Luckily, the eruption did not occur without warning. Earlier in the spring the United States Geological Survey noticed a harmonic tremor on their seismographs, meaning that magma was moving inside the volcano. Realizing that an eruption was likely, if not imminent, a hazard alert was issued, warning residents in the area of the potential catastrophe. A bulge appeared on the northwest flank of the mountain and was soon growing at a rate of six feet per day. The USGS then offered an evacuation of everyone within a five-mile radius of the volcano's base. Less than a month later, Mount St. Helens erupted, instantly taking it from relative obscurity into the international headlines.

The Niagara is a short river that runs along the United States-Canadian border, connecting Lake Erie with Lake Ontario. A few miles before it reaches Lake Ontario, the river splits in two and then, literally, drops away. The two falls, American Falls on the United States' side, and Horseshoe Falls, on the Canadian side, are separated by the small, wooded Goat Island.

∞

Horseshoe Falls is by far the larger and more powerful of the two. It is 176 feet high, 2,500 feet wide, and comprises 90 percent of the Niagara's water flow. In fact, water flows over Horseshoe Falls at the astonishing rate of 45 million gallons per minute.

American Falls is only slightly higher (182 feet), than Horseshoe Falls, yet it is much narrower (1,100 feet) and does not possess nearly the water power of Horseshoe Falls. Many geologists fear that as Horseshoe Falls erodes, it could digress into a cascade and drain the remaining 10 percent of the water flow from American Falls. Such an event will not occur for several hundred thousand years, if at all.

© Audrey Gibson

© Stan Osolinski/M.L. Dembinsky Photo Assoc.

ABOVE:

With its fine white mist, perpetual rainbows, and millions of gallons of thundering water, Niagara Falls has long been a major attraction for tourists, honeymooners, and thrill seekers. For years, fool-hardy souls entombed themselves in barrels and plummeted over the falls. A few survived, but many died, and when a large section of the falls fell away in the 1940s, barrel shooting became certain suicide. While there are many waterfalls that are taller, and at least two that carry more water, few possess the grandeur and awe-inspiring beauty of Niagara Falls.

∞

Erosion of the falls, however, is taking place. Geologists believe that they have moved a total of seven miles since their formation. They probably reached their present position about seven hundred years ago. As recently as three hundred years ago, Horseshoe Falls did not possess its distinctive horseshoe shape. Today it is estimated that Horseshoe Falls, where erosion is most prevalent, recedes about four feet every year. Erosion takes place as Niagara's water eats away at the soft limestone and shale base of the fall. When this happens, the strong dolomite rock at the top of the falls will be left unsupported and eventually become loose and crash down.

∞

Why should not we . . . have our national preserves . . . in which the bear and panther and even some of the hunter race may still exist and not be "civilized off the face of the earth." Or should we, like villains, grub them all up for poaching on our own national domains?
—Henry David Thoreau

∞

RIGHT:

It was writings such as Henry David Thoreau's that spurred Americans into action and led to the formation of Yellowstone National Park on March 1, 1872, the first national park in the world. Never before had such a huge wilderness been deemed by law as a place to be protected and cherished. Over one hundred years later, Yellowstone remains the largest national park in the world and, in many people's eyes, the most beautiful. It spans northwest Wyoming, eastern Idaho, and southern Montana.

RIGHT:

One of the unique aspects of Yellowstone is that nowhere else on earth is molten interior as close to the surface. As a result, Yellowstone boasts a collection of more than three hundred geysers, the most famous of which is Old Faithful. Adopted as the park's symbol, Old Faithful gets its name from the fact that it hasn't changed its pattern of eruption in one hundred years.

∞

Almost dependable enough to set your watch by, the geyser begins its show with a series of sporadic spurts. Then, suddenly, it blasts a plume of hot water and steam two hundred feet in the air. The blast lasts from two to five minutes, and releases as much as nine thousand gallons of water before receding into the earth.

OREGON DUNES

When traveling south from the coastal town of Florence, Oregon, you will notice that an unusual and striking phenomenon quickly comes into view—the famous Oregon Dunes. Sand dunes of this size are usually associated with places such as the Sahara Desert or the beaches of Southern California, yet here on a small, ten-mile stretch of beach in the Pacific Northwest sit some of the largest dunes in the world. With the highest ones ranging between two hundred and five hundred feet, these dunes are higher than any measured in the Sahara Desert.

© Gerry Ellis/Ellis Wildlife Collection

© Scott Blackman/Tom Stack & Associates

RIGHT AND BELOW:
Scientists believe that most of the dunes were created within the last fifteen thousand years in a process that continues today. Erosion from the sandstone mountains in the neighboring Siuslaw National Forest as well as sediment transported by rivers and streams is dumped into the ocean and deposited onto the shore. Further supplies of sand are brought to the area by the ocean currents. When the tide is out, the dry sand is picked up by wind and deposited farther inland, forming the dunes.

OPPOSITE PAGE:
It can be said that Arizona is the capital of North America's natural wonders. This dry, sweltering state is home to the Grand Canyon, Monument Valley, Blue Mesa, the Petrified Forest, and the spectacular, ever-changing Painted Desert.

(Arizona)

PAINTED DESERT

Located in the northwest corner of Arizona, the Painted Desert is an intricate network of buttes, ravines, crests, peaks, and valleys. It extends for three hundred miles between the Colorado and Little Colorado rivers, from the edge of the Grand Canyon to the Petrified Forest.

∞

As the sun begins to rise, the beauty of these badlands becomes evident. The vivid colors of the rolling crests and jagged peaks seem to glow in the rays of the low-lying sun. As the day moves on and the sun climbs higher in the sky, the brilliance and the hue of the desert seem to dull a bit. But as the sun descends in the later afternoon, the desert comes alive again in all of its Technicolor beauty.

The Painted Desert is technically a badland, like the Badlands in South Dakota. Almost completely devoid of vegetation, badlands are the result of widespread erosion from wind and rain. What makes the Painted Desert distinctive is its kaleidoscope of vivid, swirling colors, which change and shift as the sun moves across the sky. Millions of years ago, the area around the desert was ripe with volcanic activity. The mineral-rich ash from these volcanoes mixed with the sedimentary rock left by ancient seas and rivers created the beautiful reds, blues, purples, yellows, and pinks of the Painted Desert.

© Stan Osolinski/FPG International

THE PETRIFIED FOREST

Scattered amid the dry, cracked hills of Blue Mesa in the southwestern corner of the Painted Desert lies the Petrified Forest. From a distance, this loose collection of tree trunks and large logs looks like normal wood, the remnants of an abandoned lumber mill or a leveled forest. Upon closer inspection, however, it becomes apparent that they are not made of bark, wood, and sap but of solid rock—the fossilized remains of a long-extinct forest.

∞

The creation of the Petrified Forest started more than 200 million years ago, when the area was a wooded, swampy floodplain inhabited by giant dinosaurs. Many of the trees in the area reached two hundred feet or more and had diameters as wide as fifteen feet. As the trees died, they were covered with mud, sand, and ash from nearby volcanoes and sank into the swamp. The shifting of the North American plates eventually buried the logs to depths of up to one thousand feet. Silica-laden groundwater permeated the wood and turned it into colorful quartz gems such as agate, onyx, jasper, and amethyst.

∞

Although known to Native Americans for centuries, it was not seen by white men until the nineteenth century. Lieutenant Lorenzo Sitgreaves of the U.S. Army discovered the Petrified Forest—the largest collection of fossilized trees in the world, covering 94,189 acres. The local tribes believed the stone logs were either the remains of a giant named Yietso or the arrow shafts of the god Shinauv.

(Michigan)

PICTURED ROCKS

PREVIOUS PAGE:

The Ice Age, or the Pleistocene glacial epoch, is the sixth of the seven epochs of the Cenozoic era. During this time continental ice sheets ripped through large areas of North America, sculpting mountains and digging out entire valleys throughout Canada and the northern United States. The Great Lakes of North America, the largest group of lakes in the world, are a direct result of this one-million-year period of glacial activity.

∞

Lake Superior, the most northwesterly of the Great Lakes, and its surrounding areas are full of picturesque natural wonders, whose origins are either a direct or indirect result of the Ice Age. Perhaps the most visually dramatic natural wonder in the Lake Superior area is a fifteen-mile stretch of red sandstone cliffs known as Pictured Rocks.

© Stan Osolinski/M.L. Dembinsky Photo Assoc.

ABOVE:

Located in Michigan on the southern shore of Lake Superior, Pictured Rocks is a spectacular system of colorful cliffs, which rise to more than two hundred feet in some places. To say that these cliffs were caused by the glaciers is a bit misleading. When the glaciers receded and Lake Superior was formed, the steep southern shore was exposed to the erosive powers of the waves, wind, and rain. Over millions of years, elaborate caves, pillars, peaks, and sand dunes were carved out of the once-smooth cliffs.

RIGHT:

Today, most of these unusual formations are visible only by boat. Miners Castle, which lies at the end of the Pictured Rocks Trail, is the one formation that can be approached by land.

© Ian J. Adams/M.L. Dembinsky Photo Assoc.

(California)

SAN ANDREAS FAULT

I'll tell you what . . . we're having an earthquake.
—Al Michaels,
ABC Sports Broadcaster,
pregame show of the
1989 World Series

∞

One of the world's largest and perhaps most famous fault lines, the San Andreas Fault forms a twenty-mile-deep continuous fracture in the earth's crust from the coastal region of Northern California southward to the Cajon Pass, more than six hundred miles away. California has the distinction of resting where two tectonic plates meet. Much of North America lies on the American Plate, while most of California and the Pacific Ocean lie on the Pacific Plate. In essence, the Pacific Coast is moving northwest along the fault line, while the rest of the United States is moving southeast. At the current rate of movement—about two inches a year—Los Angeles will reach San Francisco's current latitude in about nine million years. In the 100 million years since the San Andreas Fault was formed, the two plates may have been displaced by as much as three hundred miles, according to scientists' estimates.

∞

A problem arises from the friction caused by these two colossal landmasses rubbing against each other. Tension builds up along the fault line and is periodically released in the form of earthquakes. Many geologists believe that several major earthquakes may occur within the next hundred years or so, forever altering the geography of California.

Earthquake Trail →

Next to Kokee State Park on the southwest section of the tiny (551 square miles) island of Kauai in Hawaii lies the 1,866-acre Waimea Canyon. This tropical canyon paradise is a series of gorges cut into the horizontal layers of old lava flows of the Kokee Plateau.

∞

© Brian Parker/Tom Stack & Associates

Known as the Grand Canyon of the Pacific, Waimea is brilliantly hued with colors that range from the blues and mossy greens of its dense vegetation to the reds and browns of the volcanic escarpment, which towers as high as 2,857 feet. The tropical greenery of the deep valleys is home to an estimated three hundred varieties of flora and fauna. While much of the terrain is too rugged for the average traveler, the canyon does contain a system of trails for those rugged enough to attempt them.

© Dennis Hallinan/FPG International

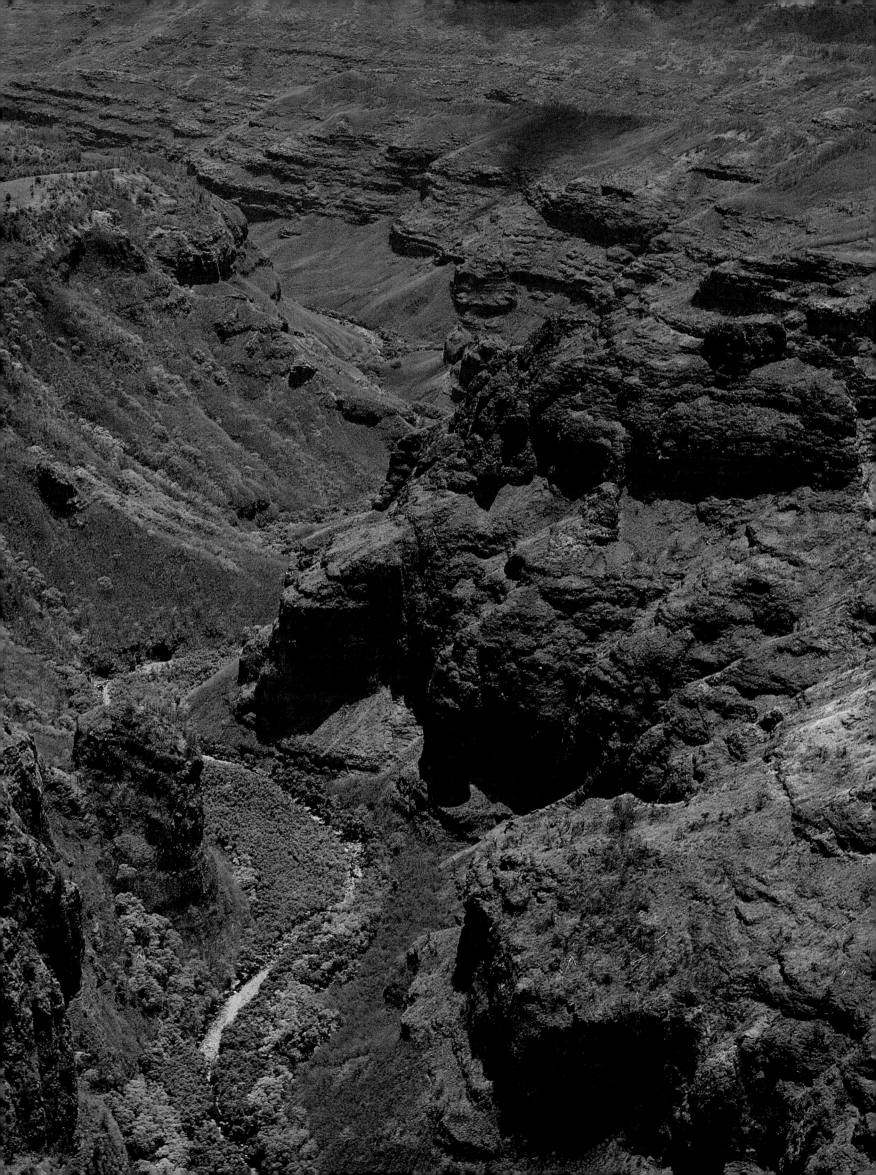

A relatively young island, Kauai was formed, like the rest of the Hawaiian islands, from volcanic activity through a fissure, or "vent," on the floor of the Pacific Ocean. Molten lava spewed out of this vent until the island was formed. The area of Waimea Canyon was once a major lava flow in the early history of the island.

After the lava cooled, the Waimea River was formed from rain runoff. It is this river that sculpted the towering crests of Waimea Canyon.

WISCONSIN DELLS

Once called Kilbourn, the city of Wisconsin Dells changed its name in 1931 hoping that the more descriptive title would attract tourists. This small Wisconsin town was formed in the 1850s when the Chicago, Milwaukee, St. Paul & Pacific Railroad extended its tracks over the Wisconsin River. Today, the town of Wisconsin Dells is primarily known as the starting point for water trips up and down an area of the Wisconsin River known simply as the Dells.

∞

According to Winnebago legend, the Dells were formed when a giant serpent moved southward, battering its way through great masses of rocks, leaving the land scarred and broken. The "serpent's path" covers three scenic landings in the Upper Dells and the picturesque Rock Island in the Lower Dells. With such colorful names as Devil's Elbow, Fat Man's Misery, Narrows, Navy Yards, Cave of the Dark Waters, Sugar Bowl, Giant Arrow Head, Grand Piano, and Hawk's Bills, the Dells are a series of architraves, sculptured cornices, molded capitals, scrolls, and fluted columns carved out to the surrounding land by the forces of the Wisconsin River.

∞

Near the Dells are seven miles of sandstone rock, some of which can be seen from the bridge that divides the Upper Dells from the Lower. Here the towering ledges of Potsdam sandstone are laced with ferns, vines, and flowering vegetation hanging from crevices in the rock walls.

INDEX